Ballerina

A Step-by-step Guide to Ballet

{ The best ballerinas practice every day and love to learn new steps. **Hiba** }

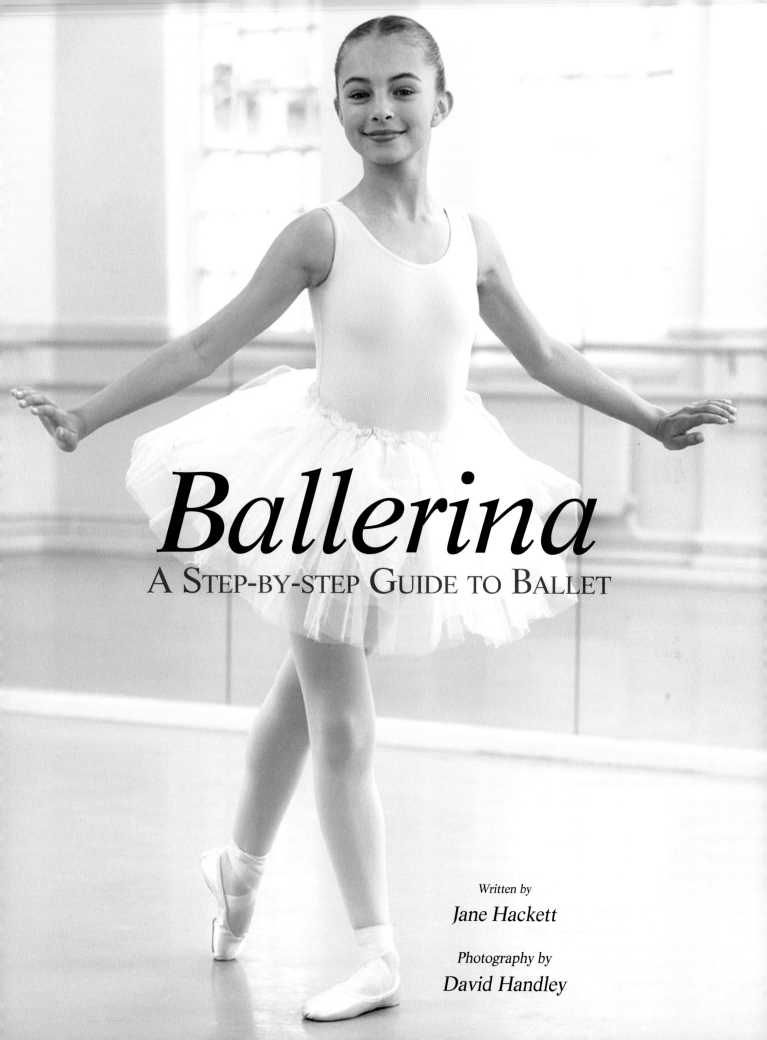

Ballerina

A STEP-BY-STEP GUIDE TO BALLET

Written by
Jane Hackett

Photography by
David Handley

Contents

Dreaming of becoming a ballerina helps me with my practice. **Frieda**

Introduction
Practice makes perfect

Ballet is beautiful to watch and satisfying to learn. It is based on ordinary movements, such as bending, stretching, sliding, jumping, and turning, which are done in a special way. As a ballerina dances, we see circles, lines, and balance in her moves. It takes time to train your body in this way and this book shows exercises and steps that will help you to do this. Ballet began in France so all the steps have French names. Ballet dancers from anywhere in the world can work together because they know these names.

This book gives a step-by-step guide to barre work, simple steps, harder steps, and performing dances. You might not be able to do it all at first, but with practice it will become easier and more enjoyable each time. The DVD shows some of the steps and dances moving to music. Just like your ballet class, the DVD will help you understand and practice the moves. Watch carefully to see the way the steps are performed and how they fit with the music.

If you dream of becoming a ballerina, regular practice is the first step to achieving your goal. As you practice, imagine the other dancers all over the world who are doing exactly the same thing and, like you, following their dream!

Jane Hackett
Director
English National Ballet School

> *I love to try and make perfect positions.* **Monique**

Barre When this symbol appears, it means that some or all of the moves on those pages feature on the DVD. The title around the symbol tells you which section of the DVD to watch. For example, this particular symbol tells you to watch the Barre section.

Ready to dance
Looking like a ballerina

Learning to look like a ballerina in class and on stage is an important part of a young dancer's training. The right clothes and hairstyle will ensure that nothing gets in your way and you can concentrate on your practice. Allow time before class to put on your dancewear and do your hair. You will soon be able to get ready quickly.

1. Ponytail

A ballerina bun

Dancer's checklist

Good dancers are well organized. It is a good idea to keep your things neatly together in a special bag so you have them all ready whenever you want to practice.

The items you will need are:

1. **Leotard, tights, and skirt**
2. **Ballet shoes**
3. **Hairpins, ribbon, comb, small mirror**
4. **A shoe bag to help keep your shoes neat and clean**
5. **A notebook and pen to keep a list of the steps you learn**
6. **A bottle of water**

What to wear

For girls, a leotard, tights, and ballet shoes are the best items to wear when you practice. You can also add a skirt. For warming up, you can wear wool legwarmers and a crossover cardigan. You should take these off when your muscles are warm. Boys can wear a T-shirt and stretchy shorts.

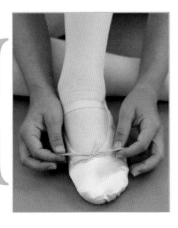

Ballet shoes

Ballet shoes can be made of leather or of shiny satin, like this pair. It is important that the shoes are a good fit to show your pointed feet. A dancer's shoes must be clean and have elastic sewn on to keep them in place. The strings at the front should be tied neatly in a bow and tucked out of sight.

Your hair should be as neat and tidy as your ballet clothes. Practice doing your hair in different ballerina styles.

2. Twist   **3. Final touch**

1. Comb your hair into a neat ponytail, fairly high on your head.
2. Twist your hair tightly around the elastic. Fix it in place with bobby pins.
3. Use a little water to smooth down any messy hair. Add a ribbon, making sure it is fixed securely.

Ballet hairstyles

Your hair should be pinned away from your face and neck. This will help to show your graceful head and neck movements and stop any hair from falling in your eyes. Dancers usually wear their hair in a bun. Sometimes younger dancers pin up their hair in braids. If you have short hair, you can wear an elastic headband around your head to keep your hair neat.

Help check your friends' hair

How to warm up
A safe start to ballet practice

A good warm-up is the best start to a ballet class. In the class, you will put your body in positions that it is not used to. Your muscles will be stretching, and your bones will bend and turn in new ways. You will lift your legs higher and bend more deeply as you try harder steps. To do this, you must start with gentle warm-ups. Each one can be repeated 10 times and stretches can be held for 10 counts.

Stretching and curling your fingers will warm up your hands so that you can make beautiful arm positions.

Sit with a straight back and neck. Push your knees down sideways with your feet together. This is called "frogs" and it will help you turn your legs out.

Hiba sits with a straight back and her stomach in

Try to stretch both your legs and your feet

Star step
The splits is a strong stretch for more advanced dancers. Frieda only tries this if she has done a long warm-up. Her legs are turned out from her hips and stretched out in a straight line, in front and behind her body.

Stretching muscles

Look after your muscles—they are important! Keep them warm at the start and end of every class. Always begin with a gentle, slow warm-up. As you repeat the positions, your muscles will get warmer and you can stretch more. You may not be able to do all the exercises at first. If you practice often, your muscles will become stronger and more flexible. Remember to breathe deeply when you stretch. You will be surprised at how much this helps your muscles.

Hiba and Olivia keep their legs in "frogs" and reach their arms forward for a stronger stretch in the hips and back.

With your hands in an open flower shape, push your hands together from wrists to fingertips and pull them apart. This will help you with your hand positions.

Jumping rope is a good warm-up, especially on a cold day! It also helps you jump without getting out of breath too quickly.

Legs are stretched from the hips down to the toes

Sit with a straight back and your legs stretched.
1. Flex your feet upward. This will help you bend and jump.
2. Stretch down across your instep and toes. This will help you point your feet.

1. **2.**

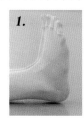 

When I have warmed up, I feel ready to jump, skip, and spin. Hiba

Frieda's feet are in first position. Her legs are turned out from the hips and her arms are in *bras bas* (arms low).

Feet & arm positions

Five positions

Shapes for your arms and legs

All the movements in ballet come from five positions. The shapes that ballerinas make with their bodies are a combination of the circles and straight lines that you will learn in these positions. For instance, your arms may be held softly in a round shape while your legs are in a strong, straight line. Whatever the position, your legs and feet should be turned out sideways.

First position

Hold your arms in a circle in front of your ribs. Turn your legs out from the top down to your heels. Don't let your feet roll inward.

Second position

Open your arms to a rounded position with the hands lower than the shoulders. Make a space between your feet as wide as your hips. Your legs should still be turned out.

{ *I try to move smoothly from one position to the next.* **Charlotte** }

Third position

One arm stays in second and the other moves to first. Your front foot is halfway across the back foot with legs together.

Third position

Demi-seconde   ## Demi-bras

In demi-seconde ("half second"), the arms are halfway between second and *bras bas* with hands curved down. In *demi-bras* ("half arms"), they are between first and second.

Fourth position

Fifth position

Lift the front arm into a round position over your head. Slide the front foot forward so there is a space between your legs.

Move both arms in a circle above your head. Cross your front foot so only the big toe of the other foot can be seen and the feet are touching.

Fourth position   Fifth position

Third, fourth and fifth positions are hard to do well. Don't worry if they take longer to learn. You need strength in your hips to keep your legs and feet turned out.

Older dancers perform basic positions en pointe

Barre work
Getting stronger every day

Dancers hold on to a handrail called a barre to support them while they practice positions. Even experienced ballerinas do barre work at the start of each class. If you don't have a barre, hold on to the back of a chair. Practice in front of a mirror sometimes, so you can check your positions. Don't worry if you can't copy all the positions straight away. As you get stronger, you will be able to hold the positions for longer. Barre exercises are the preparation for everything else in ballet.

*I try to make my pliés
graceful.* **Hiba**

Good posture is essential for
a ballerina. At the beginning
and end of each *plié*, check
that you are standing correctly,
with your stomach in and
back straight. Your shoulders,
hips, and heels should be in a
line. Remember to hold the
barre gently, not tightly.

1. Ready in first

2. Demi-plié

3. Grand plié in first

The plié positions should
flow smoothly. With your
feet in first position, hold
the barre with one hand
and look at your other
arm, which is in second.

Make a diamond shape
with your legs as your
knees bend. Keep your
heels on the ground
and let your arm float
down to *demi-seconde*.

Bend deeper and let
your heels come off the
ground. Look at your
arm as it lowers to *bras
bas*. Hold your back
straight and knees out.

*Hiba holds the
barre lightly*

First barre exercises
Demi-pliés and grands pliés

Pliés ("bends") are some of the most important moves in ballet. A ballet dancer performs *pliés* in every class. *Pliés* build strength and turnout in your legs and hip joints. They will help you with your jumps and pointe work. You will start at the barre with *demi-pliés* ("half bends") and progress to *grands pliés* (full bends).

Star step
Frieda is strong enough to do *grand plié* without the barre. This requires excellent balance.

4. Demi-plié	5. Straighten legs	6. Open out arm to finish	Grand plié in second	Grand plié in third

Push your heels back to the ground as you come up into *demi-plié* again. Keep watching your hand as it lifts to first.

Feel your thigh muscles push together and pull your stomach in as you straighten your legs. Your head should incline toward the barre.

Stand tall and feel a straight line from your heels to your head as you open your arm. Turn your head and relax your shoulders.

Your heels must stay on the ground for *grand plié* in second. This position will help you later when you do jumps in second.

Don't let your knees and feet roll forward as you come up from *grand plié* in third. Keep your leg muscles strong.

The best pliés

Pliés should be smooth and quite slow. They are usually done to adagio (slow) music. When you first learn *pliés*, you should face the barre with two hands holding on. Practice *demi-plié* first, before you try *grand plié*. Keep your legs turned out as you go smoothly down and up. This requires strength and control. You can work sideways to the barre when you get stronger and need less support. Take your hands off the barre sometimes to check your balance.

Hiba performs a beautiful *grand plié* in second. Her thighs are parallel to the floor, like a table. Her knees point out to the sides and her back is straight. She uses the barre to support her as she bends deeply into the position.

15

Ports de bras
Forward and backward

Ports de bras ("carriage of the arms") describes the way you hold and use your arms. You will begin by learning the different arm positions on their own. Later, you will combine them with feet, leg, and body positions to make a beautiful, complete movement. It is best to practice *ports de bras* at first with the help of the barre. Good dancers use their whole bodies in every movement, not just their arms and legs. A strong body will make all your positions better.

A ballerina moves her arms, legs, and body together

1. Start

2. Port de bras forward

3. Stand straight

Your back will soon become more flexible

It is important to start in a good position with your stomach in and your back straight. Breathe in and feel your body lift as your legs stretch.

Keep your back long and arm round as you stretch forward. Watch your hand, as you do when performing *pliés*. Don't let your hips push back.

Push your feet into the ground and stretch your legs as you come up straight. Your arm has moved through *bras bas* and lifted to first position.

Ports de bras really stretch my body. **Charlotte**

Hiba practises with two hands on the barre

Star step
Frieda does a full *ports de bras* to the floor, holding the barre. Her back and leg stretch forward together.

Coordination

Moving your head, arms, and body together is called coordination. When you first start to practice *ports de bras*, begin with two hands on the barre. Don't let your body twist to the sides as you go forward and back. When your sides and back are strong, you can practice sideways to the barre. The movements should flow. Good coordination will help you later with jumping and fast steps.

Keep your stomach strong

4. Stretch up

5. Port de bras back

Feel as if you are growing taller as you continue to lift your arm to fifth. This helps your spine to stretch so you can bend back in the next step.

Don't try to bend too far. Your arm should stay in fifth as you go back. End the sequence as you began, with your arm in second.

17

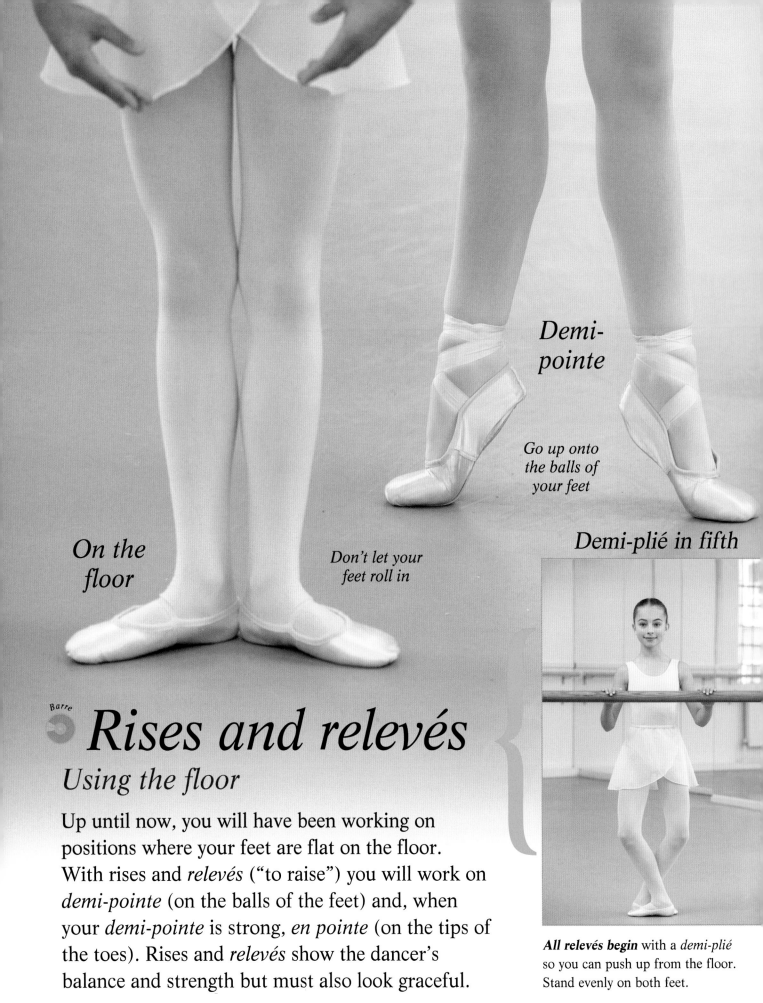

On the
floor

Demi-
pointe

Go up onto
the balls of
your feet

Don't let your
feet roll in

Demi-plié in fifth

Barre

Rises and relevés

Using the floor

Up until now, you will have been working on positions where your feet are flat on the floor. With rises and *relevés* ("to raise") you will work on *demi-pointe* (on the balls of the feet) and, when your *demi-pointe* is strong, *en pointe* (on the tips of the toes). Rises and *relevés* show the dancer's balance and strength but must also look graceful.

All relevés begin with a *demi-plié* so you can push up from the floor. Stand evenly on both feet.

En pointe

Wear special shoes for en pointe

Getting stronger

When you do a rise or *relevé*, you will show a lovely line from the top of your leg to your toes. Your legs must be strong and stretched for these positions. In rises, you push from the floor with straight legs. Your toes stay exactly where they are. For *relevés*, you always start from a *plié* and give a little spring to reach the position. Your toes will move to come underneath you. Try to keep your legs and feet turned out so your heels are forward. Later, you will do all these steps without the barre and, finally, you can try them *en pointe*.

Many years ago, dancers used rises and *relevés* to pretend that they were flying and barely touching the floor.

Rise in fifth

Relevé in fifth

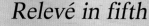

Échappé relevé to second

For a rise, stretch your knees and push up to *demi-pointe*. Lift your heels but keep your toes on the floor.

For a relevé, pull your legs and toes toward each other with a spring. Feel the stretch in your knees.

For an échappé relevé, shoot your legs out to second. The word *échappé* means "escape."

Battements
Tendus, glissés, and grands

Battement ("beating") exercises help to train your legs and feet so you can hold positions and jump high. Start with slow *battement tendu* ("stretched"), then the quicker *battement glissé* ("slide") and, finally, *grand battement* ("big"). Make sure that both your feet push against the floor as you open and close your leg. This will give you strong insteps and toes and help you get ready for pointe work.

Don't forget to lift your arm

1. Battement tendu devant

Stretch behind your knee

Stretch your instep and toes

2. Battement tendu de côté

3. Battement tendu derrière

1. *Slide your front foot devant ("front")* from first until your toes point in a line in front of your hips.

2. *Close your foot in first,* then stretch your foot *de côté* ("side"). Keep your heel forward.

3. *Close to first,* then stretch *derrière* ("back"). Both legs are turned out. Close to first and repeat *de côté*. Finish the sequence in first with your arms in *bras bas*.

Battement tendu Battement glissé Grand battement

In battement tendu, the toes point but stay *à terre* ("on the ground"). Keep both legs stretched when closing.

In battement glissé, the foot quickly slides out to a pointed position that is just off the ground.

In grand battement en l'air ("in the air"), your leg swishes through *tendu* and *glissé* to a high position.

En croix

All the *battements* should be practiced to the front (*devant*), side (*de côté*), and back (*derrière*). If you do this in a continuous sequence, it is called *en croix* ("in a cross"). You will practice many other moves *en croix*, both at the barre and in the center.

Legs and toes are stretched

{ *Good battements help me with other steps.* **Frieda** }

Star step
Frieda lifts her leg high on **grand battement**. Don't try to go too high at first. It is more important to think about the position of your legs. Your hips should not be twisted. Stretch through your legs and arms.

Your supporting foot pushes against the floor

21

Développés

Balance and strength

Développé ("unfold") exercises help with the *adage* (slow work) that comes later in the class and also with your balance. *Développé* should be slow and controlled and may require a lot of practice. Try to let the positions follow each other in a continuous, smooth movement. Think about unfolding and closing your arms and legs together.

Keep both hips facing forward

Développé derrière

This *développé* unfolds behind you (*derrière*). The sequence passes through two well-known positions in ballet: *attitude* and *arabesque*. In *attitude*, you stand on one leg with the other raised and bent at the knee. In *arabesque*, the raised leg is stretched out completely. You will have to let your body tilt forward a little as you move from *attitude* to *arabesque*.

1. Cou de pied

Place one foot above your ankle. This position is *cou de pied* ("neck of the foot").

2. Retiré derrière

Slide your foot up behind your knee. This is *retiré derrière*. Keep your knee to the side and your foot pointed.

3. Attitude derrière

With your knee lifted and hip down, unfold to *attitude derrière*, a position seen in many ballets.

1. Retiré devant

2. Unfolding

3. Développé in second

Développé to second

1. Slide your toes up your leg to under your knee (*retiré devant*). Lift your arm to first position.

2. Keep your hips forward as you unfold your leg and arm to second.

3. Unfold your leg completely. Stay balanced and stretched.

Open your arm and leg together

Développé devant

1. Attitude devant

2. Unfolding

1. Slide your foot up to *retiré* then lift it in front of you with your knee bent (*attitude devant*). Keep your lifted knee turned out.

2. As you unfold your leg, keep your thigh lifted until both knees are straight.

4. Arabesque

Now unfold completely to *arabesque*. Remember to keep your knee lifted and turned out as you unfold.

> *I can feel all my muscles working hard in développé.*
> **Charlotte**

23

More ports de bras
Flowing movements

You have already practiced *ports de bras* at the barre but it can also be performed in the center of the room. You will learn more about center practice later in the book. Remember to be slow and careful as you go through the positions. You should move smoothly, in a graceful manner.

1. **Lift one arm to first and look at your hand.** *2.* **Turn your head. Open your arm out.**

Elegant movements

Whenever you practice, do not just think about your arm and leg positions, but also about the other things that help to make these moves truly beautiful. Let your eyes follow the movement of your body, keep your neck long, and smile!

Make one smooth, flowing port de bras

1. Chassé en arrière

2. Start your circle

3. Transfer your weight

Demi-plié in fifth and slide your foot back to fourth. This slide is a *chassé en arrière* ("chase backwards"). Lift your arms to first. Make sure your weight is evenly spread on both feet.

Start to move your weight onto your back foot. Watch your front arm as you begin to draw a circle with your arms around your head. Keep your knees out.

Take your weight onto the back foot and stretch this leg as you point the other foot *devant*. Your hands and arms continue to draw a circle around you.

3. Lift the other hand to first.

4. Bring your arms to second position.

5. Let your arms float down to *bras bas*.

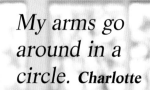

Head, eyes, and arms together

Frieda practices her *port de bras*. She keeps her legs still and moves her arms. She follows the movement of her arms with her head and eyes. Her arms float into position and she keeps her shoulders stretched as she opens out.

4. Stretch behind

Keep your stomach strong and your front foot pointed. Imagine a thread running from your foot to your top finger as you make a circle around your body.

5. Finish the circle

Change your arms over your head and finish the circle to the side. Keep your legs strong while your arms are changing. Your head also makes a circle, as you watch your hands.

6. Transfer your weight forward to finish

Arabesques
Beautiful lines

The *arabesque* is one of the most beautiful positions in ballet. The dancer makes straight lines with her legs and arms, stretching out into space like a star. Try to make your arabesques look light and easy, even if they feel difficult. You should look as if you might take off and fly away at any moment.

Focusing your eyes on one point will help you balance

First arabesque

Balance

To do a good *arabesque*, you must remember to turn out your legs and feet, stretch your legs, point your toes, and keep your stomach muscles strong. Using your back muscles will help you to keep both hips forward and to make beautiful lines with your legs and arms. Try to feel that your legs and arms are stretching out from the middle of your body.

Second arabesque

Third arabesque

Look at the pictures of the first, second, and third *arabesques*. In the first *arabesque*, the foot of the extended leg is on the ground (*à terre*). The second and third *arabesques* are *en l'air* with the leg "in the air." Look at the different arm positions of each *arabesque*.

Développe into arabesque allongée ("long")

1. Begin in *attitude* with arms in first.

2. Unfold to *arabesque*. Stretch arms and legs.

3. Stay stretched. Bend your other leg (*plié*).

{ *Arabesque is my favorite position.* }
Laurretta

Perfect balance and control

Dancers stretch at the barre to increase their flexibility.

Arabesque penchée

In arabesque penchée ("tipped"), the body tips forward as the leg lifts to make a high line. You will need strong balance, flexibility, and lots of practice to do this advanced step.

Directions of the body

Ouvert **En face** **Croisée**

When your teacher tells you to perform a move, she may want to be specific about the direction you should be in. *Ouvert* ("open") means that you face one corner in an open position. *En face* means "facing the front". In *croisée* ("crossed"), you face the other corner.

Stand evenly on both feet before you begin

1. Demi-plié in fifth

Go into demi-plié in fifth and lift your arm to first. Make sure that your knees open wide to the sides. Your weight should be balanced evenly on both legs so that you could move either foot easily.

2. Extend to side

Stay in a low demi-plié and *tendu* (stretch) your front foot to the side as you open your arms to second. Your weight is over your supporting side, while the toes of your front foot touch the ground lightly.

Center practice
Moving in different directions

Until now you have mainly been practicing with the barre. You will also do exercises in the center of the room. These will be performed in various directions, as well as moving around the room. Focus on your head, arm, and neck positions as you do not have the barre for support.

Star step
Frieda practices *temps lié en avant* ("moving forward"). Her position is *croisée* (crossed to the front) and she is just about to step *en pointe*.

Temps liés

One important exercise you will do in the center is changing your body weight from foot to foot. This linked sequence is called *temps lié* ("linked count"). Slow, careful practice is good at first. It will improve your balance and will help you to do quicker, moving steps.

{ Always start and finish well. **Charlotte** }

3. Demi-plié in second   4. Transfer weight   5. Close to fifth

Place your heel down and bend your knee while moving your body weight between your legs. You are now in *demi-plié* in second with both knees turned out. This will help to strengthen your legs.

Transfer your body weight onto the other foot and stretch the opposite leg. Hold the arms in a still second position while your body and legs are changing. Remember to stretch your instep and toes.

Feel that you are growing taller as you close back to fifth with your extended foot in front and arms in *bras bas*. The sequence should be performed smoothly, with your arms and legs moving at the same time.

Moving gracefully

An elegant ballerina

Look directly at your audience

It is important to think about the way you move as well as making sure your moves are accurate. To be a good ballerina you need to move and perform gracefully. Begin with a basic step so you can focus on how graceful you can be.

Walk and point

Ballerinas always walk and run gracefully with their legs and feet stretched in front of them. The walk and point exercise will help you with this. Move slowly and smoothly so that you stretch your legs and feet on each walk. Show your turned out legs and pointed feet. You can do this exercise faster as you get better at pointing. Eventually, the walks will become running steps.

1. Walk

Swish your front foot forward and point your toes just off the ground before you step forward.

2. Walk

Repeat the swish with your other foot. Stretch your leg and then step forward.

3. Point

Take another step forward and let the pointed foot rest lightly on the floor.

{ *I hold my arms elegantly when I walk and point.* **Olivia** }

{ A curtsey says "thank you" to the audience. *Frieda* }

Enchaînements

At first you will practice the same moves over and over again. Once you have perfected individual moves, you can try mixing them in a sequence or *enchaînement* ("chain"). See if you can make an *enchaînement* combining the walk and point moves on the opposite page with the step and curtsey below. Pay particular attention to the poses that you hold in walk and point, and the pose you hold when you curtsey in step and curtsey. Remember to be graceful!

1. Step

Step to the side and open your arms to second. Stretch one leg and foot in second position. Look at your audience.

2. Curtsey

Bring the stretched foot behind you and bend deeply. Keep balanced by putting your back foot on *demi-pointe*.

Frieda's back foot is stretched

Moving faster
Steps and enchaînements

On the next pages, you will see many different moving steps and jumps. They will start off fairly simply and gradually get more complicated. When you have practiced each step, try mixing them together in sequences or *enchaînements*. Different steps need to be danced in different ways. For instance, walks and runs should be small and neat. Remember to think about this as you are practicing. Most importantly, have fun learning and combining these steps!

Spring point

Begin a spring point by jumping one foot out to *point tendu devant* with your arms in fifth. Then spring in the air and change feet. Your supporting leg will land in a *plié* after each spring.

1. Derrière

Petit jeté derrière with arms in *demi-seconde*. This whole sequence should stay *sur place* ("in the same place").

> Change feet each time you jump.
> **Olivia**

Small jumps

Spring points, coupés, petits jetés

The small jumping steps you will learn are very alike. They are made up of positions you have learned at the barre, like *tendu*, *demi-plié*, and *cou de pied*. Practice until you have good *ballon* ("bounce"). When you know the steps, you can put them together in an *enchaînement*.

Coupé sequence

In *coupé* ("cut"), you put one foot exactly in the place of the other as you take that foot away. The *coupés* below are done with a spring on each one. As you repeat this sequence, you will find that the *tendu* at the end stretches to a different side each time. This is included in Dance 1 on pages 60–61 and on the DVD.

2. Devant

Take a spring and land with the other foot *devant*. This is a *coupé*. You should be on the same spot.

3. Derrière

Coupé back to *derrière*. Hold your arms lightly in *demi-seconde*, as if over a tutu (ballet dress).

4. Point tendu en plié

Extend the back foot to *tendu* to second *en plié*, without a spring. Look toward your foot.

Petit jeté

In a *petit jeté* ("little throw"), you jump from foot to foot. The lifted foot is pointed and touches your calf muscle. Keep your knees out and stay on the same spot as you change feet.

Petit allegro

Gallops, soubresauts, and changements

Allegro is the name given to all the jumping steps in ballet. The word means "quick and lively," which tells you the feel of the steps. Some steps you have already learned can be called *petit allegro* (small, quick steps). You will start with *petit allegro* to prepare your legs and feet for bigger jumps.

Keep your feet and legs stretched on each jump

Quick springs

Whether you perform a gallop, *soubresaut* ("sudden leap") or *changement* ("changes"), you should always aim to show a straight position in the air with legs and feet stretched and together. These are not big jumps; they are quick, with a little spring on each one. Remember to stretch your feet quickly.

{ *The music helps me jump.* **Hiba** }

1. Start

Start your gallop by swishing your front foot forward. This leg will lead on the gallops. It is turned out and stretched. Hold your arms in fourth position.

2. Gallop

Bring your legs and feet together as you spring into the air on the first gallop. Make sure that you do not jerk or strain your arms as you jump into the air.

3. Swish

Land with a demi-plié and swish your front leg forward for the next gallop. You can practice sequences of gallops before combining them with other steps.

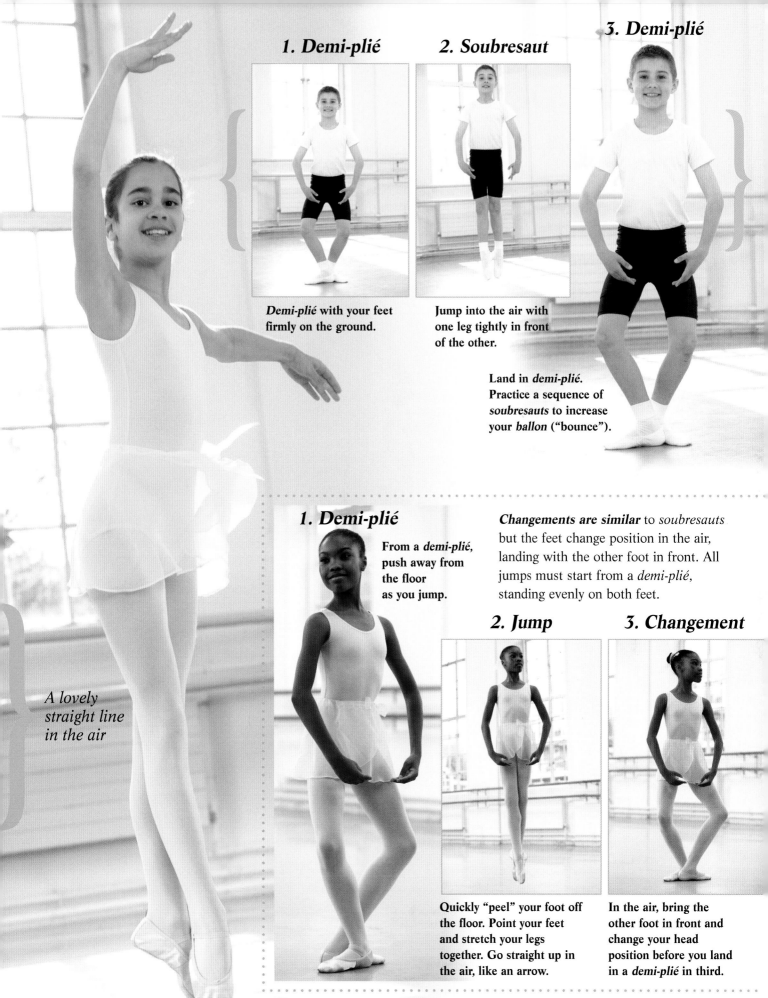

1. Demi-plié

2. Soubresaut

3. Demi-plié

Demi-plié with your feet firmly on the ground.

Jump into the air with one leg tightly in front of the other.

Land in *demi-plié*. Practice a sequence of *soubresauts* to increase your *ballon* ("bounce").

A lovely straight line in the air

1. Demi-plié

From a *demi-plié*, push away from the floor as you jump.

Changements **are similar** to *soubresauts* but the feet change position in the air, landing with the other foot in front. All jumps must start from a *demi-plié*, standing evenly on both feet.

2. Jump

3. Changement

Quickly "peel" your foot off the floor. Point your feet and stretch your legs together. Go straight up in the air, like an arrow.

In the air, bring the other foot in front and change your head position before you land in a *demi-plié* in third.

Échappés
Positions in the air

Échappé means "to escape." Instead of your legs staying tightly together in the air, as in a *soubresaut*, they open out or "escape" into another position. You will have to jump high to give yourself time to bring your legs together and then open them out while still in the air.

Ben knows that his starting and finishing positions are important. A strong *demi-plié* will help him to jump high on the *échappé*. Finishing in a *demi-plié* gives a safe landing.

1. Jump from third

Jump straight up from your *demi-plié*. Lift your arms from *bras bas* to first as soon as you leave the ground.

Échappés sautés

Échappés can be done on *demi-pointe* (page 19) or jumped in the air (*sauté*), as on this page. *Échappé sauté* has two parts to the movement. The legs move to an open position in the air and land in a *demi-plié* in that position (second or fourth). The second part of the movement is to jump up in the open position, close the legs in the air, and return to the starting position.

> I breathe in as I jump high.
> **Charlotte**

1. Straight up

Demi-plié to begin and jump straight up before opening to fourth *en l'air* with the arms in third. Charlotte is just starting to open her legs to fourth and her arms to third.

2. Demi-plié in fourth

Land in fourth in *demi-plié* with your knees turned out in line with your feet. This arm position is called "third in opposition" because the arm in front is the opposite side to the foot in front.

2. Second en l'air

Open your legs to show second position *en l'air* ("in the air"). Take your arms from first to second to match your legs.

3. Demi-plié in second

Land in demi-plié in second. To finish this sequence, you would jump up to second again, close in the air, and land in third to finish.

3. Fourth en l'air

Use the power of your landing to push straight back up in the air in the open position. Your legs are in fourth *en l'air*. Then bring your legs together. You have to be quick to fit this in while you are in the air.

4. Demi-plié close

Land back into a neatly crossed fifth position. The *échappé* will be part of a sequence and a good ending or close helps you go straight into the next step. This step has a bouncy feel.

Elegant arms and head as you jump

Pas de bourrée
Small, quick steps

Pas de bourrée takes its name from a 17th century French dance (*bourrée*). It has three quick little steps in the middle of the move that have to be fitted into one count of music.

Star step
Frieda practices her *pas de bourrée en pointe*. She also adds a *port de bras* to match the steps.

Varieties

There are many different *pas de bourrée*. The name of each one tells you how to move your feet. For instance, in *pas de bourrée derrière*, you close the same foot behind you each time. In *pas de bourrée piqué*, you "pick" up or lift your legs.

Pas de bourrée derrière

1. Tendu

Start in plié and stretch or *tendu* one leg out to the side. This is your preparation for the three steps that follow. Hold your arms in second throughout.

2. Fifth on demi-pointe

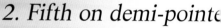

Stretch your supporting leg and rise onto *demi-pointe* as you close your stretched leg behind into fifth on *demi-pointe*. This happens in one quick movement. Make sure your feet are crossed.

Pas de bourrée piqué

1. Start | 2. Piqué | 3. Change | 4. End

Begin in cou de pied (foot just above ankle). This foot is ready to take the place of the other in the next step.

Step onto your raised foot in *demi-pointe* and lift the other foot so that it is in *retiré devant*.

With one sharp step, change your leg positions. Move your arm position from third to second.

Close your raised foot in front. Bring your arms back to third but to the other side.

3. Step to second | 4. Close in fifth | 5. Demi-plié in fifth

Open the front foot out to second on *demi-pointe*, ready for the next move. Think about the openess of this position even when your practice gets faster. Keep your arms lightly held in second.

Stay on demi-pointe and close your back foot into fifth position again. For steps 2, 3, and 4, imagine your legs are closed, open, and then closed. These three steps are done quickly.

Lower into demi-plié in fifth. Steps 4 and 5 happen almost in one quick move. From this position, you could stretch the back foot out to repeat the whole sequence.

Balancés

Waltz steps

Balancé is an elegant move made up of three small steps that stay close to the ground. *Balancés* are often mixed with bigger steps in a sequence or *enchaînement*. They are called waltz steps because, like a waltz, they are danced to a beat of three counts with one move per count.

When you are performing a balancé, the most important thing is to feel the 1-2-3 rhythm. Using the DVD can help you with this. Step 1 is strong and steps 2 and 3 are lighter. This page shows *balancé de côté* ("to the side").

Practice balancés in different directions

1. Down

2. Up

3. Down

Step to one side with a *demi-plié.* The arms move to the same side in third position. Incline or lean your head in the direction that you have stepped. This is your strongest step.

Step onto demi-pointe on your back foot and lift the front foot to *cou de pied* (just above the ankle). This is the up move. The rhythm for *balancé* is down–up–down.

The third step is like the first one but this time it stays on the spot. Let your body move to the side and your head will follow. Bend low into the *demi-plié.*

Look along your arm

{ *It took me time to learn how to do a balancé.* **Monique** }

Balancé and ports de bras

In this sequence, Monique is doing *balancé en avant* ("forward") and then *en arrière* ("backward"). To do this well, you must carefully practice stretching your feet on each little step. Match your *port de bras* and head positions to the moves. Let your arms and head lift when you go forward and bend low when you step backward. You will use the *balancés* on these pages in the dances on the DVD.

1. Down...

Monique swishes her left foot forward as she steps onto it in *demi-plié*. Arms are in *arabesque*.

2. Up....

Step up onto your right foot on *demi-pointe*. Your left foot is in *cou de pied*. Keep your eyes up.

3. Down...

Step down onto your left foot again with your right foot in *cou de pied* behind the ankle.

4. Down....

Step back on the right foot. Swish the left foot behind the ankle. Change your arms to third.

5. Up...

Lift the right foot to *cou de pied*. Look downward.

6. Down...

Step down on your right foot and raise the left foot so that it is behind your ankle.

Stretch your feet on each step

{43}

Look at a fixed spot in front of you and start to turn your body. Keep your eye on the spot. Whip your head around and find the spot again as you start to come back to the front.

Find a spot   **Fix your eyes**   **Whip your head**

1. Demi-plié in fourth

From tendu in second, move to *demi-plié* in fourth, bringing your stretched leg behind you. Fix your eyes on a spot in front of you.

Put your hands on your shoulders to help your balance

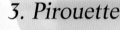

Turning steps
Spotting and pirouettes

There are many turning steps in ballet. In addition to remembering your arm and leg positions, you need to learn a technique called "spotting." This will stop you from getting dizzy as you turn, especially if you are doing several turns in a row.

Pirouettes

One of the best known turns in ballet is called a *pirouette* ("whirl"). In a *pirouette*, you spin around while balanced on one leg. *Pirouettes* can be done with different arm and leg positions. Advanced *pirouettes* can be done in *arabesque, attitude,* or *en pointe.*

2. Relevé devant

Lift your back foot to *relevé devant* (raised in front). Push into the *relevé.* Close your arms into first. This will help you start to turn.

3. Pirouette

Push your knee to the side as you turn your body. Hold your arms steady in first. This will support your back. Keep spotting.

4. Complete the turn

Bring your eyes back to your spot as you turn to the front. Close in *demi-plié* in fifth with arms *bras bras.*

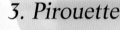

1. Tendu	2. Transfer	3. Close

From a *demi-plié*, extend (*tendu*) one of your legs to second position.

Quickly transfer your weight and stretch your other foot.

Close your stretched foot in front. Do several *glissades* in a row, gradually getting quicker.

Glissade

Glissade ("slide") is a small, quick step on the ground that brings both feet together. It is often followed by a jumping step, like *assemblé*. Practice each move separately. Eventually, you will be able to do it in one quick movement.

Assemblé

Assemblé ("assemble") is an *allegro* step that shows both legs coming together in the air. *Assemblés* can move forward, back, or to the sides.

1. Demi-plié

2. Swish

In an assemble derrière, it is the back foot that swishes out and the same foot that lands behind. Start in third position for both your arms and feet.

Push your front foot into the floor as you stretch the back foot out to the side. Stretch the arms from third to open *arabesque*.

Glissades and assemblés

Joining steps together

In an *enchaînement*, you will perform lots of different steps in a continuous sequence. To keep your dance smooth, you must include some smaller steps on the ground, like *glissades*, to join together the jumps and position *en l'aire*, like *assemblés*. *Glissades* and *assemblés* are used together in many famous ballets.

In *assemblé*, bring the feet and legs together so that they join tightly. Both feet should land at the same time.

3. Together

As you jump, bring in the foot that is on the floor to join the extended foot. Remember to think about your stretched legs and feet.

4. Land

Finish in demi-plié. Look toward your raised arm. Practice this *assemblé* sequence until you are able to perform it in one quick, light movement.

Jetés
Bigger jumps

There are many different kinds of *jeté* and you have already learned about *petits jetés*. These pages show how to do a *jeté* and a *grand jeté* (a big *jeté*). A *jeté* is a jump from one leg to the other. *Jeté* means "to throw" and in a simple *jeté*, your leg swishes, or "throws," out and you jump onto it. In a *grand jeté*, you must do a big "throw" to start the movement followed by a really big jump onto that leg.

Practicing jetés

It may take some practice before you can do a smooth sequence of *jetés*. *Battements glissés* and *grands battements* at the barre will help you with the throwing movement. Try to move smoothly from the starting position of a *demi-plié* to the jump. You should change legs when you are *en l'air*. You may need to practice the leg movements separately, but it is important to include your arms and head positions as soon as you can.

{ *Practicing the splits helps me with my grand jeté.* **Frieda** }

1. Swish

Start from a *demi-plié* in third and your arms also in third. Swish your back foot out.

2. Jump

Jump high in the air. This is when your feet change. Bring the stretched leg under you and fold the other foot behind.

3. Land

Land on your front leg. Keep your back leg raised and touching the calf.

This is called jeté derrière. Practice a sequence of these. Make them follow smoothly, one after the other. Push your feet against the ground as you swish out on the first move. This will help to stretch your feet when you jump.

The legs are fully stretched in grand jeté

As you jump, remember to stretch your feet and legs in the air. This gives the steps the right shapes and also makes them easier to do.

Grand jeté

Frieda is doing a *grand jeté*. This is a step for advanced dancers. The dancer jumps from one leg and lands on the other. Frieda throws or *jetés* her front leg so that her legs are in the splits when she is in the air. She lands safely in *demi-plié* on her front leg. To help make her jump even higher, she lifts her head and arms and looks toward her high arm. This is an exciting move that is often used in ballets.

Pas de chat

Coordinating body, arms, and legs

If you have seen a cat lightly jump with all its feet in the air and then delicately land, you will have a good idea of how to do a *pas de chat* ("cat step"). It is quite a difficult move because the legs lift quickly one after the other so it is important to practice the different positions of your arms and legs slowly. You will need coordination to move different parts of your body at the same time. The exercise below will help you to prepare for a *pas de chat*.

Pas de chat are fun to do and fun to watch!

1. Retiré one side	2. Retiré other side	3. End

Start with your feet and arms both in third position. Lift your back foot to *retiré derrière*. *Pas de chat* always begins with the back foot.

Swap your arms and legs so your front foot is in *retiré devant* and your arms are on the other side. Keep your knees turned out.

Close your foot back to third. This is your landing position. This exercise will help you to feel the exact position that your legs should be in a *pas de chat*.

Timing

A good *pas de chat* is all about timing. You must lift one leg and then the other, as you have practiced. When you land, one leg should also follow the other. You must aim for your feet to be crossed in the air. *Pas de chat* is a very quick step and usually happens on one count of music.

{ *I love to feel both feet in the air.* }

Charlotte

A perfect pas de chat!

Monique practices lifting both her legs, one after the other.

Bend your second leg in quickly

Star step
Practice doing sequences of *pas de chat*. Move across the room and land lightly like a cat. Check in the mirror to see if your feet come neatly together on each *pas de chat*.

En pointe
Rises and relevés

Ballerinas started to dance *en pointe* (on the tips of the toes) over 150 years ago. When you dance *en pointe*, you wear special shoes that support your toes and feet. You must not start pointe work until you have been learning ballet for some time, and not before you are 11 years old. The moves on these pages will be ones you have already learned, but now you will work *en pointe*.

Pointe shoes

Pointe shoes are made from layers of cloth and glue. They are baked hard in a special oven and then covered in pink satin. They can be dyed different colors to match your costume but are usually the same color as your tights. Your first pointe shoes should be very carefully fitted to suit the shape of your foot. When ballerinas are performing, they need at least one new pair of pointe shoes every week.

Wearing pointe shoes for the first time is exciting!

1. Demi-plié in first

To do a relevé en pointe, start as you would in *demi-pointe* with a *demi-plié*. When you first wear pointe shoes, your *pliés* will feel differently!

2. Relevé in first

The feet and toes pull toward each other as you *relevé en pointe*. Your feet and legs are turned out. Feel your muscles stretch.

How to tie pointe shoes

1. Ballerinas keep their pointe shoes in place with ribbons. Take one of the ribbons around your ankle.

2. Wrap the inside ribbon fully around your ankle. Make sure your ribbons are long enough to do this.

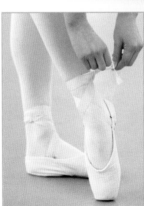

3. Wrap the outside ribbon in a circle around your ankle, too. The ribbons will be crossed at the front.

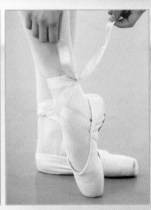

4. Tie the ribbons in a double knot on the inside of your ankle, just behind the bone. Make sure it is secure.

5. Tuck the ends neatly out of sight behind the ribbons. Make sure the ribbons are not tied too tightly.

Rise in first

Relax your shoulders and neck

To do a rise en pointe, start from first position. Lift your heels and keep your toes where they are. Push hard against the floor as you rise to help you get *en pointe*.

Relevé in fifth

In relevé in fifth en pointe, one leg is crossed tightly in front of the other. The toes and feet move to come together tightly, unlike in a rise. Hold the barre to support you but do not push into it.

Échappé to second

1. Start in *demi-plié* with your feet firmly on the floor. Your arms are in first.

2. Shoot your legs out to second *en pointe*. Open your arms out to second too.

3. In one movement, close to *demi-plié* in fifth with the other foot in front.

53

Posés and soutenus
Turning steps

Many turning steps can be both done on *demi-pointe* and *en pointe*, including *posé* ("step") turns and *soutenus* ("turns"). Before doing any turning steps *en pointe* in the center, you must practice exercises at the barre to strengthen your feet and balance. Remember to keep your feet and knees turned out. This page shows you how to practice *posés* at the barre.

The barre helps you to balance

1. Prepare

Slide one foot out to second until the foot comes just off the floor. At the same time, *demi-plié* on the supporting leg. The raised foot must be stretched and ready for you to step onto it.

2. Posé derrière

Step onto your pointed foot with a straight leg and quickly bring the other leg to *retiré derrière*. Bring your body over your supporting leg. The Star step on the opposite page shows you how a *posé* looks with a turn added.

The raised foot can be held *devant* (in front) or *derrière* (behind). Here, it is *devant*.

Soutenu

1. Relevé in fifth *en pointe.*
2. Start to turn. As you get halfway around, the back foot comes to the front.
3. Continue to turn until you have completed the circle.

1. Relevé

2. Turn toward the back foot

3. Complete the turn

Soutenu en pointe

When you perform a *soutenu en pointe*, you spring into *relevé* from *demi-plié* in fifth. The arms must move with the legs. You use the energy from this move to make the turn happen. Don't put too much force into the move and control the end of the turn so you can carefully lower off pointe. When you are turning on the small tips of your pointe shoes, you turn faster than you do on *demi-pointe*.

{ *I use spotting on soutenu.* **Charlotte** }

Star step
Frieda does a sequence of *posé* turns across the room. She must spot in the direction that she is moving. She can do these on *demi-pointe* or *en pointe*.

Keep your legs and feet together

Dances
Preparing for performance

You have learned positions, barre exercises, simple steps, and harder steps. You have also seen how to combine the steps into *enchaînements* or sequences. The next section is the most enjoyable of all! You will get to put the *enchaînements* together to make a whole dance. The next few pages will show you how to change simple sequences into interesting dances to perform on stage. Once you have learned the dances and added your finishing touches, like costumes and hairstyles, you will be ready for your performance!

From class to stage
Stage directions and floor patterns

The goal of learning all the steps and sequences is to put them together in beautiful dances. The choreographer (the person who arranges the dances) will tell you the steps you have to perform and the different directions in which you have to perform them. Dancers learn names for these directions and also for the different places on the stage.

Ballerinas spend hours perfecting their dances

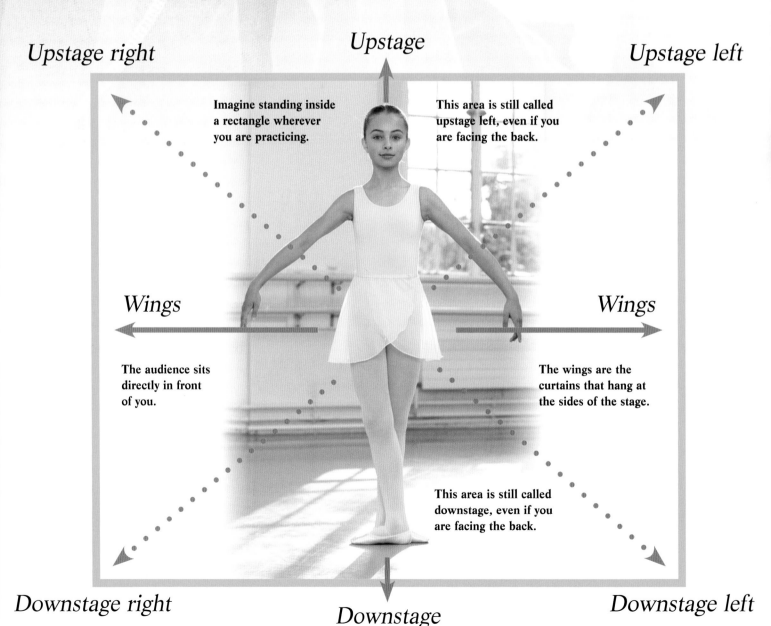

Upstage right

Upstage

Upstage left

Imagine standing inside a rectangle wherever you are practicing.

This area is still called upstage left, even if you are facing the back.

Wings

Wings

The audience sits directly in front of you.

The wings are the curtains that hang at the sides of the stage.

This area is still called downstage, even if you are facing the back.

Downstage right

Downstage

Downstage left

Choreography

On these pages and the following ones you will learn about the different ways dancers make patterns around the stage. When you have read these pages and watched the dances on the DVD, try making up your own dances. Choose a piece of music and decide which steps match the music. Join the steps into *enchaînements* and choose the direction in which each section should move. Teach the dance to a friend to check that your dance is clear. This is your first choreography.

Floor patterns

The directions in which the steps move and the pattern that this makes on the stage are carefully planned. This is called the floor pattern. The dancers keep this pattern in their heads but sometimes they they will write it down. It is important that a dancer shows clear patterns, lines, and circles as she moves and that she knows exactly where she is going. This makes the dance look beautiful. It is especially important to have a clear floor pattern when a lot of dancers are performing together.

Hiba gallops en diagonale

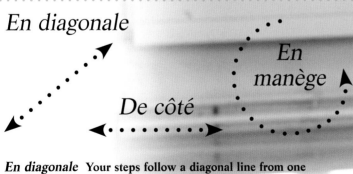

En diagonale

De côté

En manège

En diagonale Your steps follow a diagonal line from one upstage corner to the opposite downstage corner.

De côté Your steps move to one side or the other. You can also do this with your back to the audience (facing upstage).

En manège Your steps take you around in a circle. Remember to look in the direction that you are moving.

Dance 1
From practice to performance

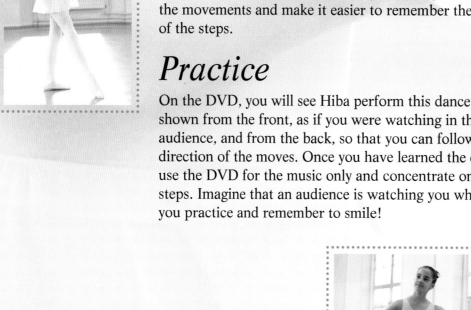

Starting out

All the steps in both Dance 1 and Dance 2 (pages 62–63) are shown in the book. These dances are also shown on the DVD. Sometimes it is easy to do the steps alone and much harder to join each sequence together smoothly. Look at the floor pattern that has been drawn to help you and watch the dance through on the DVD a few times. If you find something difficult, go back to the book and check how to do the step. It is very important to dance with the music. It will help you to give the right feel to the movements and make it easier to remember the order of the steps.

Practice

On the DVD, you will see Hiba perform this dance. It is shown from the front, as if you were watching in the audience, and from the back, so that you can follow the direction of the moves. Once you have learned the dance, use the DVD for the music only and concentrate on the steps. Imagine that an audience is watching you when you practice and remember to smile!

Following the floor pattern

Look at the floor pattern below while watching Dance 1 on the DVD. The numbers refer to the steps that you have to do and these are listed next to the floor pattern. It is a lot to think about but the more you watch the DVD, look at the floor pattern, and practice, the easier it will become.

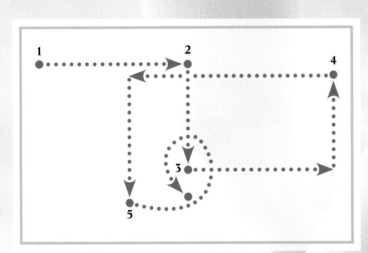

Key
R = right L = left Fwd = forward

Dance
Start upstage R corner, facing side, R foot pointed *devant* in 4th

1 – 4 gallops with R, arms 4th

2 – 4 gallops with L, arms 4th
Step R and *temps levé* with L leg raised *devant*
Step L and *temps levé* with R leg raised *devant*
Step R with 3 *temps levés* with L leg raised *devant*
3 *petit jetés* L, R, L and *temps levé*
3 *petit jetés* R, L, R and *temps levé*
3 spring points R, L, R, step onto R and curtsey

3 – 4 gallops with L, arms 4th
4 gallops with R, arms 4th
Step L and *temps levé*, step R and temps levé
4 *petit jetés* L, R, L, R, with ¼ turn to face the opposite side

4 – 4 gallops with L
4 gallops with R
Step L and *temps levé*, step R and *temps levé*
Step onto L and curtsey
3 *coupés*, point L, 3 *coupés*, point R
3 *coupés*, point L, 3 *coupés*, point R
3 *petit jetés* R, L, R and *temps levé*, with ½ turn to face back
3 *petit jetés* L, R, L and *temps levé*, with ½ turn to face front
3 spring points L, R, L

5 – Step onto L foot and curtsey
A big step onto R, L foot behind, arms lift to 5th
Run in a small circle *en manège*, turning toward L hand, finishing in the same spot
Step L into *arabesque*, balance
Chassé R foot fwd and cross arms on chest to finish

Dance 2
A more advanced dance

Dancing gracefully

Dance 2 has harder steps. This dance is also shown on the DVD. Once you have learned the sequence, make sure your head and arm positions are elegant on each move. You can check this in a mirror when you practice. As you follow the floor pattern and think of the directions of your moves, remember to turn out and stretch your legs. Don't worry if it seems a lot to remember at once. Ballet dancers spend weeks practicing for a performance until they hardly have to think which step comes next.

Performance style

Imagine what your audience will see when they watch your dance. The following things will make your performance really special and interesting for you to dance and for your audience to watch.

• Vary the way you move. For example, *balancé* is smooth and flowing, *pas de chat* is light and quick, *glissade* is small and sharp, and *assemblé* shows a long shape in the air.
• Remember to change your head and body positions with different steps.
• Dance exactly with the music and change the mood of your steps as the music changes.
• Use the whole of the room or stage as you follow the floor patterns.

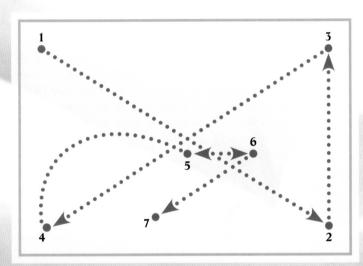

Key

R = right L = left fwd = forward
rpt = repeat

Dance

Start upstage R corner, L foot pointed behind, arms *demi-seconde*

1 – *En diagonale* moving toward downstage L corner:
Balancé fwd and back L, R, L, R
Balancé side to side L, R, L, R
Balancé fwd and back L, R, L, R

2 – Run up to upstage L corner, facing *en diagonale* to downstage R corner, standing on L foot, R foot pointed behind, arms *demi-seconde*

3 – *En diagonale* moving toward downstage R corner:
Balancé fwd and back R, L, R, L
Balancé side to side R, L, R, L
Balancé fwd and back R, L, R, L

4 – Run toward R in small semicircle to center
Stand, feet in 5th, R foot front

5 – *Glissade derrière* to L, *jeté derrière* onto L
Glissade derrière to R, *jeté derrière* onto R
2 slow *petits jetés* L, R, *pas de chat*, *changement*
Glissade derrière to R, *assemblé* over
(swish R foot out and close in front)
Glissade derrière to L, *assemblé* over
(swish L foot out and close in front)
Tendu à la seconde with L foot, *demi-plié*
4th behind with L, *pirouette*, close L foot behind
Relevé devant with R, *relevé derrière* with L, *relevé devant* with R
Step back onto L, with R foot pointed *devant* facing *croissée* (downstage diagonal), arms in 3rd

6 – 3 *posés* on *demi-pointe en diagonale*, close in 5th
Relevé 5th, arms 5th, close

7 – *Pas de bourrée derrière*, *pas de bourrée devant*
Relevé 5th, *soutenu* turn toward back (L) foot
Finish L in front, lower heels
Open back foot to wide 4th position, front leg *en plié*, arms in *arabesque*, facing downstage corner

Dancing together
Moving with a friend

After you have learned and mastered the different positions and steps yourself, it is fun to do them with a friend. This will make your dance more interesting to perform and watch. If you are dancing with a partner, you should move together and make your positions as similar as possible.

Support each other

Working with a partner means that you can do things that you could not do on your own. Blake helps Charlotte to jump high and to keep her balance as she leans back. Blake supports Charlotte but she cannot have him do all the work. She must be strong in her movements, too. The support your partner gives is the same light support that you get from the barre.

1. Charlotte holds Blake's hand as she does a *petit jeté*. Blake's feet are firmly on the ground.

2. She pushes down on his hand to jump high on the *temps levé* (a hop on one foot).

3. Blake supports Charlotte as she lands and stretches back. They smile out at the audience.

Sequences

Olivia and Hiba are repeating a sequence of *petits jetés* and *temps levés*. They transfer their weight from one side to the other in the *petit jetés* and then hop into the air (*temps levé*). They have to hold hands lightly and must not lean on each other as they transfer their weight.

Hiba and Olivia stretch their feet as they hop and point their toes in *temps levé*. They move their heads at the same time and in the same direction.

Pas de deux
A dance for two

All the famous ballets include a *pas de deux* for the ballerina and her partner. With a strong partner, the ballerina can balance for longer, jump higher, and perform more pirouettes. The dancers must remember to focus on their own movements as well as their positions with their partner.

Frieda is *en pointe* in *relevé*.

Ben helps Frieda balance in *arabesque*.

Ben supports Frieda as she stretches back.

Working in pairs

The dancers must have trust and confidence in each other to perform well together. They have to concentrate, because some of the difficult moves can be dangerous if performed incorrectly. Older ballet students have *pas de deux* classes to learn how to work with a partner. A ballerina must be strong *en pointe* and have good balance. Male dancers do fitness training so they can lift and support their partners.

Graceful lines

Two dancers can make beautiful lines
and positions together. The lines of Ben
and Frieda's arms and legs make a
balanced shape. The way the performers
look at each other and dance together
can tell us a story. For instance, if Frieda
is playing a fairy, Ben will touch her
gently and lift her very high, as if
she is as light as a feather.

*I train hard to be
a good partner.* **Ben**

**Ben and
Frieda look at
each other as
they dance.**

*Both dancers
make the same
pose with their
arms*

Mime

Story without words

We use mime every day, for instance, when waving "hello" to a friend. In ballet, there is no speaking so dancers use mime to tell the story. These moves are done in a way that makes them clear to see and easy to understand. The mime stories in some ballets have been done in the same way for over 100 years.

Be clear

It is important to use big, clear movements and to hold each position for a few seconds so that everyone can see and understand. Remember to include your whole body and face in the mime. Simply changing your expression, from a happy face to an angry face, can tell a very different story.

I...   *see...*   *you!*   *You...*

1. Olivia moves her hand toward the center of her chest to say "I."

2. She points her finger first to one eye and then to the other to say "see."

3. Olivia points at Hiba to say "you." Another way to do this is to extend your hand outward.

4. Now it is Hiba's turn to reply. She looks angry as she points back.

Frieda is miming crying.
She inclines her head slightly to
show that she is sad and keeps her
movements clear.

{ *I like to make up mime stories.* **Olivia** }

go away!

I am sad

Let's be friends again!

5. She stretches her hand and arm as if pushing
her friend away. She turns her face away, too.
Olivia looks sad.

6. Olivia moves her fingers down
her cheeks to show that tears are
falling and she looks down sadly.

Please...

Listening

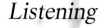

Cup your hand softly behind your ear, turning your head so your audience can see.

Asleep

Put your hands together and your head on one side, as if you were lying on a little pillow.

1. Clasp your hands together and stretch them outward as if you were pleading or asking for something.

Love

Bring your hands in to touch just below your heart. Make sure both your elbows are lifted.

Anger

Bend your arms at the elbow and clench your fists. Remember to look angry.

Death

Lift your arms crossed over your head with clenched fists. Bring your arms down strongly in front of you.

Storytelling
Traditional moves

All the famous ballets, such as *Swan Lake*, *Sleeping Beauty*, and *Giselle*, include long mime sequences for each character. These sequences tell us the story and are easy to understand. The way the mime is set to the music also helps us understand the story. For example, if the music is sad, the mime will be sad.

bless...

2. Lift both arms to the side and let them float softly downward as if the hands were gently touching something.

the baby

3. Bend your arms toward you as if you were holding a baby. Don't forget to look at your baby.

Keep your positions away from your body

Engagement

Point to your ring finger to show that you will be married.

Practicing mime

Perform the moves as if you were on stage. They must be big enough for hundreds of people to see and understand. All the moves should be done elegantly in the style of a ballerina, with legs turned out, a long neck, and hands and head lightly in place. If you are playing a character role, such as an old lady or a shy child, then you must move to suit the part. Remember to make sure the expression on your face matches the mime.

Simple makeup

Ballerinas wear makeup on stage so that the audience can see their faces clearly. A little bit of makeup on your eyes, lips, and cheeks will make your face clear under the bright lights. Young dancers should keep their makeup very natural and not too heavy.

Getting ready

Hair, makeup, and costume

It is fun to dance for yourself but it is even better to dance for an audience. Whether it is in your room or a real theater, a show needs costumes and makeup. They will help you feel like a real ballerina and they can play an important part in telling a story, too.

A simple ribbon and skirt can turn your practice clothes into a costume

Ask a friend to help you with your makeup and hair. You can try different ballerina hairstyles and see what eye and lip colors suit you best. Use a long mirror to check that your costume and hair are neat and tidy. Once you are finished, help your friend to get ready.

Decorations for your hair turn a simple bun or braids into a beautiful ballerina style. The shining beads will sparkle on stage against the lights.

{ *A costume makes me feel special.* **Monique** }

Preparation

Enjoy trying out lots of ballerina hairstyles and different makeup and hair accessories. For each ballet performance, you will have to wear different costumes and style your hair and makeup in different ways, so the more you practice now, the better prepared you will be.

For some performances you may get to wear a headdress or tiara. You should put your headwear on whenever you practice so that you can get used to wearing it. Anything added to your hair or costumes must be fixed in place so that nothing will drop off when you are doing fast moves, especially pirouettes.

Performance

Finishing touches

Watching a ballet performance can be magical. Some of the magic comes from the costumes and makeup that a dancer wears. A ballerina takes great care when getting ready for a performance to make sure her hair, costume, and makeup are perfect.

The dancers practice the curtsies and bow that they will do at the end of the performance. The girls have their back foot pointed. Everyone moves at the same time.

How to do a bun

1. Brush your hair up from your neck into a high ponytail.

2. Twist the ponytail so that all your hair is included in the twist.

3. Start to pin the twist in a circle around the elastic.

4. Tuck the ends in to complete the circle; fix with bobby pins.

5. Put a hairnet over the bun so that no hairs will come loose.

6. Add a clip or ribbon for decoration. Fix it firmly with bobby pins.

Ready to dance

Frieda wants to be a professional ballerina. It is a wonderful job to have but takes a lot of practice and hard work. Frieda is training full-time and has already performed with English National Ballet. She arrives early at the theater each evening to prepare for the performance. She can get ready quickly because she has practiced so many times.

How to apply stage makeup

1. Use foundation or powder that is close to your skin color.

2. Add eyeshadow. Pick a color that suits your eyes.

3. Eyeliner and false eyelashes will make your eyes look bigger.

4. Blush on the cheekbones highlights the face on stage.

5. Finally, add lipstick for your finishing touch.

{ *At last, I dance in costume.* }
Frieda

Ribbons and headdresses help to complete your ballet outfit

Younger dancers wear natural makeup

Charlotte wears a tutu for the first time

The younger dancers look forward to being able to perform in full costume.

Being a ballerina

The younger children in this book dream of becoming dancers. They go to ordinary schools and attend ballet classes after school. Frieda is already at full-time ballet school and Laurretta will start soon. If you too dream of becoming a ballerina, daily practice will help your dream come true.

{ *Glossary*

A

allegro Quick, lively movements. In ballet, this is the name given to jumped steps.

arabesque A ballet position with extended, stretched arms and legs.

assemblé to assemble or bring together. A ballet step that brings both legs together in the air.

à terre On the ground.

attitude A ballet position with rounded arms and a bent raised leg.

B

balancé A waltz step danced on the count of three.

ballon Bounce. This term is used to describe the correct way to do little jumps in ballet.

barre A long horizontal handrail that dancers use for support when practicing.

battement Beating. A straight, strong action of the leg used in many exercises and steps.

bras bas Arms low. A low, round position of the arms used for resting or finishing movements.

C

changement Changes. A small jump that changes feet.

chassé To chase. A small, sliding step. When done in a sequence, one foot chases the other.

choreography Putting steps together to make a dance.

coordination Moving different body parts at the same time.

cou de pied Neck of the foot. A position where the toes of one foot touch the other ankle.

coupé To cut. A move where one foot takes the place of the other.

croisée Crossed. A position where the body is slightly turned and the audience will see the legs crossed.

curtsey A smooth movement as the knees bend and the head lowers. It is used to show respect or the end of something and is often done at the end of a ballet.

D

de côté To the side.

demi-bras Half arms. A position where arms are held halfway between first and second position.

demi-plié Half bend. A small bend with the feet flat on the floor.

demi-pointe Half pointe. A position where you stand on the balls of the feet, halfway between the floor and full pointe.

demi-seconde Half second. A position where arms are held lower than second position, as if resting on a tutu skirt.

derrière Behind.

devant In front.

développé To unfold. The name of a smooth, unfolding movement of the leg.

downstage The area of space between the center of the stage and the audience.

E

échappé To escape. A movement where the legs open at the same time.

en arrière Moving backward.

en avant Moving forward.

enchaînement A chain. A sequence of linked steps.

en croix In a cross. A sequence of moves that go to the front, the side, and the back.

en diagonale On a diagonal.

en face Facing the front.

en l'air In the air.

en manège Originally a circus ring. A series of steps performed in a circle.

en pointe Dancing in special shoes on the tips of your toes.

G

gallop A traveling step where you bring your feet together when you are in the air.

glissade To slide. A quick step on the ground that brings both feet together.

grand jeté Big throw. The name of a high jump that moves from one leg to the other.

grand plié Big bend. This is a full bend of the knees with the body upright.

I

instep The arch that is in the middle of your foot.

J

jeté To throw. A jumping step that starts with one leg "thrown" out and lands on the other.

O

ouvert Open. A position where you face one corner of the stage and the audience will see an open position.

P

pas de bourrée A step named after a French dance (*bourrée*) with quick, small steps.

pas de chat Cat steps. A light jump with the feet taking off and landing one after the other.

Glossary

pas de deux Step for two. A dance for two people.

petit allegro Small, quick jumps.

petit jeté Little throw. A springing step from foot to foot.

piqué To pick up. A step that lifts the foot quickly.

pirouette To whirl. A turning step performed on one leg.

plié A bend in the knees. (see also *demi-plié, grand plié*)

port de bras Carriage of the arms. A sequence of arm positions.

posé Step. A step onto a flat foot, on *demi-pointe* or full pointe.

posture The way in which you stand.

R

relevé To raise. A quick movement onto *demi-pointe* or pointe.

retiré To take away. A position with one raised foot touching the other knee.

rise A lifting of the heels.

S

soubresaut A sudden leap. A jump with the legs held tightly together in the air.

soutenu A turn that changes feet.

spotting The technique of using the eyes to focus on a spot as you turn. This stops you from getting dizzy.

spring point A jumping step that extends one leg out and then the other.

sur place In the same place.

T

temps levé Lifted count. A hop.

temps lié Linked count. A step that moves one leg and then the other with a transfer of weight.

tendu To stretch. Usually, one leg in a stretched position.

turnout The basic position of the legs in ballet, with the legs turned out from the hip joint down to the feet.

tutu A ballet dress with a skirt made of layers of net.

U

upstage The area of space between the center of the stage and the back.

W

wings The curtains that hang at the side of the stage.

{Index

Acknowledgments

DK and the author would like to thank: Frieda, Charlotte, Monique, Hiba, Olivia, Laurretta, Blake, Ben, and Nic for being such brilliant ballet dancers; their families, and their teachers and schools: Valerie Hitchen, Susan Robinson, Francis Holland School, and the Royal Opera House's Chance to Dance; Victoria Vaughan and the staff at English National Ballet School for their assistance; Zoë Uffindell and all the staff at Khaki Production for their tremendous work on the DVD; Heather Scott and Richard Glasstone for proofreading; Lindsay Kent for help on the photo shoot. **For further information, go to www.enbschool.org.uk and www.ballet.org.uk.**

LONDON, NEW YORK, MELBOURNE, MUNICH, AND DELHI

Brand Manager & Senior Designer Lisa Lanzarini
Project Editor Laura Gilbert
Design Assistance Mark Richards
Publishing Manager Simon Beecroft
Category Publisher Siobhan Williamson
Production Editor Jonathan Ward
Production Controller Amy Bennett
DVD Production Khaki Production
US Editor Margaret Parrish

First published in the United States in 2007
by DK Publishing
345 Hudson Street
New York, New York 10014

14 10 9 8 7 6 5
014 – BD316 – 01/08

DK books are available at special discounts when purchased in bulk for sales promotions, premiums, fundraising, or educational use. For details, contact: DK Publishing Special Markets, 345 Hudson Street, New York, New York 10014 SpecialSales@dk.com

A catalog record for this book is available from the Library of Congress

ISBN: 978-0-7566-2668-6

Color reproduction by MDP Ltd.
Printed and bound in China by South China Printing Co. Ltd

Discover more at
www.dk.com